The Thriving Business Journal

Reflect

Analyze

Grow

For more small business resources visit:
SmallBusinessSarah.com

Get your FREE
Simple Strategies to Save your Business Money Checklist at:
https://www.SmallBusinessSarah.com/savemoney

How to use This Journal

The format of this journal is undated weekly prompts, for all 52 weeks in a year. Three of the prompts are directed and one is free form.

Every four weeks there is an opportunity to review past business goals, and set new goals for the following four weeks.

But first, begin by reflecting on the overall mission and values of your business, and by setting some goals for the entire year.

Begin with Purpose

My Business Purpose

My Business Values

My Business Mission Statement

Make a plan for your business and enable success.

My Business Hours

My Business Work Space

My Business Routine

My Business Goals for this Year

Action Steps to Take

My Business Goals ~ Next Four Weeks

Action Step to Take

Week 1

What is my intent for _____?

If my week goes exactly as planned, I will finish…

In my business, I am most looking forward to…

Other thoughts for my week to come…

Week 2

List 5 ways to bring excitement to my
business this week.

My number one priority this week is…

Who can I thank this week for helping my business grow or providing a useful resource?

Other thoughts for my week to come…

Week 3

What business task can I eliminate or hire out to create more focused time?

I want to find help this week with...

If _____ could be easy, it would look like…

Other thoughts for my week to come…

Week 4

My favorite discovery last week was…

This week my business needs me to…

I want my business to be known for…

Other thoughts for my week to come…

Review of Business Goals

What were my accomplishments?

What did I learn?

What worked well, what didn't?

My Business Goals ~ Next Four Weeks

Action Steps to Take

Week 5

I can serve others through my business this week by…

The biggest change I need to make in my business is…

I will connect with two people this week.
They are…

Other thoughts for my week to come…

Week 6

The best thing about my business is…

This week, I need to learn more about and research…

An opportunity I couldn't pass up would be...

Other thoughts for my week to come...

Week 7

When people ask me about my business, I love to tell them…

A resource I would like to explore for my business is…

I can point _____ (who?)
towards this opportunity…

Other thoughts for my week to come…

Week 8

Others tell me I am most helpful when…

A fun project I would like to explore this
week is…

I am grateful that my business…

Other thoughts for my week to come…

Review of Business Goals

What were my accomplishments?

What did I learn?

What worked well, what didn't?

My Business Goals ~ Next Four Weeks

Action Steps to Take

Week 9

My best business tip is…

My work life balance is…

This _____ (book, product, podcast, video, etc.) was super helpful to my business because…

Other thoughts for my week to come…

Week 10

List 10 ways to accomplish _____.

What will readers/customers gain from my latest…

I can love my business this week by…

Other thoughts for my week to come…

Week 11

If I were to dream big for my business then…

This week I want to create for my business…

What if I…

Other thoughts for my week to come…

Week 12

I define business success as...

In my business, I least enjoy...

My biggest business challenge right now
is…

Other thoughts for my week to come…

Review of Business Goals

What were my accomplishments?

What did I learn?

What worked well, what didn't?

My Business Goals ~ Next Four Weeks

Action Steps to Take

Week 13

What is my intent for _____?

If my week goes exactly as planned, I will finish…

In my business, I am most looking forward
to…

Other thoughts for my week to come…

Week 14

List 5 ways to bring excitement to my business this week.

My number one priority this week is…

Who can I thank this week for helping my business grow or providing a useful resource?

Other thoughts for my week to come…

Week 15

What business task can I eliminate or hire out to create more focused time?

I want to find help this week with…

If _____ could be easy, it would look like…

Other thoughts for my week to come…

Week 16

My favorite discovery last week was…

This week my business needs me to…

I want my business to be known for...

Other thoughts for my week to come...

Review of Business Goals

What were my accomplishments?

What did I learn?

What worked well, what didn't?

My Business Goals ~ Next Four Weeks

Action Steps to Take

Week 17

I can serve others through my business this week by…

The biggest change I need to make in my business is…

I will connect with two people this week.
They are…

Other thoughts for my week to come…

Week 18

The best thing about my business is…

This week, I need to learn more about and research…

An opportunity I couldn't pass up would
be…

Other thoughts for my week to come…

Week 19

When people ask me about my business, I love to tell them…

A resource I would like to explore for my business is…

I can point _____ (who?)
towards this opportunity…

Other thoughts for my week to come…

Week 20

Others tell me I am most helpful when…

A fun project I would like to explore this week is…

I am grateful that my business...

Other thoughts for my week to come...

Review of Business Goals

What were my accomplishments?

What did I learn?

What worked well, what didn't?

My Business Goals - Next Four Weeks

Action Steps to Take

Week 21

My best business tip is…

My work life balance is…

This _____(book, product, podcast, video, etc.) was super helpful to my business because…

Other thoughts for my week to come…

Week 22

List 10 ways to accomplish _____.

What will readers/customers gain from my latest…

I can love my business this week by…

Other thoughts for my week to come…

Week 23

If I were to dream big for my business then…

This week I want to create for my business…

What if I…

Other thoughts for my week to come…

Week 24

I define business success as…

In my business, I least enjoy…

My biggest business challenge right now is...

Other thoughts for my week to come...

Review of Business Goals

What were my accomplishments?

What did I learn?

What worked well, what didn't?

My Business Goals - Next Four Weeks

Action Steps to Take

Week 25

What is my intent for _____?

If my week goes exactly as planned, I will finish…

In my business, I am most looking forward to…

Other thoughts for my week to come…

Week 26

List 5 ways to bring excitement to my business this week.

My number one priority this week is…

Who can I thank this week for helping my business grow or providing a useful resource?

Other thoughts for my week to come...

Week 27

What business task can I eliminate or hire out to create more focused time?

I want to find help this week with…

If _____ could be easy, it would look like…

Other thoughts for my week to come…

Week 28

My favorite discovery last week was…

This week my business needs me to…

I want my business to be known for…

Other thoughts for my week to come…

Review of Business Goals

What were my accomplishments?

What did I learn?

What worked well, what didn't?

My Business Goals ~ Next Four Weeks

Action Steps to Take

Week 29

I can serve others through my business this week by…

The biggest change I need to make in my business is…

I will connect with two people this week.
They are…

Other thoughts for my week to come…

Week 30

The best thing about my business is…

This week, I need to learn more about and research…

An opportunity I couldn't pass up would be…

Other thoughts for my week to come…

Week 31

When people ask me about my business, I love to tell them…

A resource I would like to explore for my business is…

I can point _____ (who?)
towards this opportunity…

Other thoughts for my week to come…

Week 32

Others tell me I am most helpful when…

A fun project I would like to explore this week is…

I am grateful that my business…

Other thoughts for my week to come…

Review of Business Goals

What were my accomplishments?

What did I learn?

What worked well, what didn't?

My Business Goals - Next Four Weeks

Action Steps to Take

Week 33

My best business tip is…

My work life balance is…

This _____(book, product, podcast, video, etc.) was super helpful to my business because...

Other thoughts for my week to come...

Week 34

List 10 ways to accomplish _____.

What will readers/customers gain from my latest…

I can love my business this week by…

Other thoughts for my week to come…

Week 35

If I were to dream big for my business then…

This week I want to create for my business…

What if I...

Other thoughts for my week to come...

Week 36

I define business success as…

In my business, I least enjoy…

My biggest business challenge right now
is…

Other thoughts for my week to come…

Review of Business Goals

What were my accomplishments?

What did I learn?

What worked well, what didn't?

My Business Goals ~ Next Four Weeks

Action Steps to Take

Week 37

What is my intent for _____?

If my week goes exactly as planned, I will finish…

In my business, I am most looking forward to…

Other thoughts for my week to come…

Week 38

List 5 ways to bring excitement to my business this week.

My number one priority this week is…

Who can I thank this week for helping my business grow or providing a useful resource?

Other thoughts for my week to come…

Week 39

What business task can I eliminate or hire out to create more focused time?

I want to find help this week with…

If _____ could be easy, it would look like…

Other thoughts for my week to come…

Week 40

My favorite discovery last week was…

This week my business needs me to…

I want my business to be known for...

Other thoughts for my week to come...

Review of Business Goals

What were my accomplishments?

What did I learn?

What worked well, what didn't?

My Business Goals ~ Next Four Weeks

Action Steps to Take

Week 41

I can serve others through my business this week by…

The biggest change I need to make in my business is…

I will connect with two people this week.
They are…

Other thoughts for my week to come…

Week 42

The best thing about my business is…

This week, I need to learn more about and research…

An opportunity I couldn't pass up would be…

Other thoughts for my week to come…

Week 43

When people ask me about my business, I love to tell them…

A resource I would like to explore for my business is…

I can point _____ (who?)
towards this opportunity…

Other thoughts for my week to come…

Week 44

Others tell me I am most helpful when…

A fun project I would like to explore this
week is…

I am grateful that my business…

Other thoughts for my week to come…

Review of Business Goals

What were my accomplishments?

What did I learn?

What worked well, what didn't?

My Business Goals ~ Next Four Weeks

Action Steps to Take

Week 45

My best business tip is…

My work life balance is…

This _____(book, product, podcast, video, etc.) was super helpful to my business because...

Other thoughts for my week to come...

Week 46

List 10 ways to accomplish _____.

What will readers/customers gain from my latest…

I can love my business this week by…

Other thoughts for my week to come…

Week 47

If I were to dream big for my business
then…

This week I want to create for my business…

What if I...

Other thoughts for my week to come...

Week 48

I define business success as…

In my business, I least enjoy…

My biggest business challenge right now
is…

Other thoughts for my week to come…

Review of Business Goals

What were my accomplishments?

What did I learn?

What worked well, what didn't?

My Business Goals ~ Next Four Weeks

Action Steps to Take

Week 49

My best business tip is…

My work life balance is…

This _____(book, product, podcast, video, etc.) was super helpful to my business because…

Other thoughts for my week to come…

Week 50

List 10 ways to accomplish _____.

What will readers/customers gain from my latest...

I can love my business this week by…

Other thoughts for my week to come…

Week 51

If I were to dream big for my business then…

This week I want to create for my business…

What if I…

Other thoughts for my week to come…

Week 52

I define business success as…

In my business, I least enjoy…

My biggest business challenge right now is...

Other thoughts for my week to come...

Review of Business Goals

What were my accomplishments?

What did I learn?

What worked well, what didn't?

My Business Goals ~ Next Year

Action Steps to Take

Get your FREE Simple Strategies to Save your Business Money Checklist at:

https://www.SmallBusinessSarah.com/savemoney

And don't forget to order another journal for next year!

Made in the USA
Las Vegas, NV
19 May 2021

23308269R00079